Informing the legislative debate since 1914 _____

The Temporary Assistance for Needy Families (TANF) Block Grant: A Primer on TANF Financing and Federal Requirements

Gene Falk
Specialist in Social Policy

January 27, 2014

Congressional Research Service

7-5700

www.crs.gov

RL32748

Summary

The Temporary Assistance for Needy Families (TANF) block grant provides federal grants to the 50 states, the District of Columbia, American Indian tribes, and the territories for a wide range of benefits, services, and activities. It is best known for helping states pay for cash welfare for needy families with children, but it funds a wide array of additional activities. TANF was created in the 1996 welfare reform law (P.L. 104-193).

TANF provides a basic block grant of $16.5 billion. It also requires states to contribute in the aggregate from their own funds at least $10.4 billion for benefits and services to needy families with children—this is known as the maintenance-of-effort (MOE) requirement. States may use TANF and MOE funds in any manner "reasonably calculated" to achieve TANF's statutory purpose. This purpose is to increase state flexibility to achieve four goals: (1) provide assistance to needy families with children so that they can live in their own homes or the homes of relatives; (2) end dependence of needy parents on government benefits through work, job preparation, and marriage; (3) reduce out-of-wedlock pregnancies; and (4) promote the formation and maintenance of two-parent families.

Though TANF is a block grant, there are some strings attached to states' use of funds. Most TANF requirements apply to families receiving cash assistance (essentially cash welfare). Families must be financially needy and have a minor child to qualify for assistance; states determine the exact financial eligibility rules and benefit amounts. Some families have eligible children but the adults who care for their children are ineligible for aid. These are termed "child-only" families because benefits are paid only on behalf of the children.

TANF work requirements generally apply to families with an adult recipient (excluding most child-only families). States must meet TANF work participation standards or risk a reduction in their block grant. The law sets standards stipulating that at least 50% of all families and 90% of two-parent families must be "engaged in work," but these statutory standards are reduced by credits for caseload reduction and state spending in excess of what is required under the TANF MOE. These credits and the effective (after credit) participation targets vary by state and year. Activities countable toward a family being counted as "engaged in work" are focused on employment or working off the cash benefit, or are intended to rapidly attach welfare recipients to the workforce; education and training is countable, but limited.

Federal TANF funds may not be used for a family with an adult who has received assistance for 60 months. This is the five-year time limit on welfare receipt. However, up to 20% of the caseload may be extended beyond the five years for reason of "hardship," with hardship defined by the states. Additionally, states may use funds that they must spend to meet the TANF MOE to aid families beyond five years.

TANF work participation rules and time limits do not apply to families receiving benefits and services not considered "assistance." Such benefits and services include child care, transportation aid, state earned income tax credits for working families, activities to reduce out-of-wedlock pregnancies, activities to promote marriage and two-parent families, and activities to help families that have experienced or are "at risk" of child abuse and neglect.

Contents

Tables

Contacts

Introduction

The Temporary Assistance for Needy Families (TANF) block grant provides federal grants to the 50 states, the District of Columbia, American Indian tribes, and the territories for a wide range of benefits and activities.[1] It is best known as the major source of funding for cash welfare for needy families with children. However, federal law allows TANF funds to be used for other benefits and services that provide economic help to low-income families with children and to support the goals of reducing out-of-wedlock pregnancies and promoting two-parent families. The TANF block grant was created in the 1996 welfare reform law (P.L. 104-193).

At the federal level, TANF is administered by the Department of Health and Human Services (HHS). However, benefits and services are provided by the states. TANF programs operate in all 50 states, the District of Columbia, Puerto Rico, Guam, and the Virgin Islands. American Samoa is eligible to operate a TANF program, but has not opted to do so.[2] Federally recognized Indian tribes may also operate TANF programs. Tribal TANF programs are funded through allocations made from the TANF basic block grant to the state in which the tribe offers TANF benefits and services.

This report provides an overview of TANF financing and rules for state programs, describing

- federal TANF grants and state funds under a "maintenance-of-effort" (MOE) requirement;

- how states may use federal TANF and state MOE funds to help achieve the purpose and goals of the TANF block grant;

- rules that apply to states when they use TANF or MOE funds to provide cash welfare to needy families with children;

- rules that apply to states when they use TANF or MOE funds for benefits and services *other* than cash welfare;

- certain accountability requirements that apply to states, including requirements that states submit plans and report data to the federal government; and

- provisions of TANF law not directly related to grants to states, such as competitive grants for promoting healthy marriage and responsible fatherhood, tribal TANF provisions, and research funds.[3]

For a less technical discussion of TANF, see CRS Report R40946, *The Temporary Assistance for Needy Families Block Grant: An Introduction*, by Gene Falk.

---

[1] This report generically refers to TANF grantees as "states," though the grantee may be the District of Columbia, tribes, or territories. TANF requirements generally apply uniformly to the 50 states, District of Columbia, and the territories. Tribal TANF programs operate differently. See "Tribal TANF" discussion later in this report.

[2] American Samoa was also eligible to operate the pre-1996 program, Aid to Families with Dependent Children (AFDC), but did not have such a program.

[3] For current data and statistics on the TANF block grant, see CRS Report RL32760, *The Temporary Assistance for Needy Families (TANF) Block Grant: Responses to Frequently Asked Questions*, by Gene Falk.

Federal Grants and State Funds

Though TANF is called a block grant, it has a relatively complicated financing system. Currently, there are two sources of federal funding for the states: the basic block and contingency (recession-related) grants. Additionally, states are required to spend a certain amount of their own funds on specified TANF-related activities for needy families with children. Therefore, the TANF financial "system" consists of both federal and state funds.

Additionally, there is federal funding for research, demonstrations, and technical assistance for "healthy marriage promotion," and competitive grants for "responsible fatherhood" initiatives. These funds (which may go to other entities, as well as to states) are discussed in "Other TANF Provisions," later in this report.

Federal TANF Funds

Table 1 shows TANF funding for FY2006 through FY2014

Table 1. Federal TANF Funds: FY2006-FY2014

(in millions of dollars)

	2006	2007	2008	2009	2010	2011	2012	2013	2014
State family assistance grant	$16,489	$16,489	$16,489	$16,489	$16,489	$16,489	$16,489	$16,489	$16,489
Supplemental grants	319	319	319	319	319	211			
Healthy marriage/responsible fatherhood grants	150	150	150	150	150	150	150	150	150
Grants to the territories	78	78	78	78	78	78	78	78	78
Grants for tribal work programs	8	8	8	8	8	8	8	8	8
Regular contingency funds	93	59	428	1,107	212	334	612	610a	610a
Emergency contingency funds				617	4,383				
Totals	17,137	17,103	17,472	18,768	21,639	17,270	17,337	17,335	17,335

Source: Congressional Research Service (CRS).

a. P.L. 112-275 appropriated $612 million to the TANF contingency fund for FY2013 and FY2014 and reserved $2 million for each year for a commission on child abuse and neglect fatalities. Thus, $610 million is available for FY2013 and FY2014 contingency fund grants.

Federal TANF funds are considered "mandatory spending" in the federal budget. The grants are *entitlements* to the states—the law entitles states, tribes, and territories to a specified amount of funding. The law specifically states that TANF does not entitle individuals to benefits and services.

Basic Block Grant

The 1996 welfare reform law entitled states to a basic TANF block grant equal to peak expenditures for pre-TANF programs during the FY1992-to-FY1995 period.[4] The mid-1990s were a period when the cash welfare rolls were at their all-time high; the block grant amount is based on federal expenditures on the cash welfare, emergency aid, and job training programs for cash welfare families that existed in that period. The basic block grant is legislatively fixed—that is, it does not change when the cash assistance caseload decreases or increases, nor is it adjusted for inflation.

Table 2. TANF Basic Block Grant to the States

State	Dollars in Millions	Percent of Total, 50 States and District of Columbia
Alabama	$93.3	0.6%
Alaska	63.6	0.4
Arizona	222.4	1.3
Arkansas	56.7	0.3
California	3,733.8	22.6
Colorado	136.1	0.8
Connecticut	266.8	1.6
Delaware	32.3	0.2
District of Columbia	92.6	0.6
Florida	562.3	3.4
Georgia	330.7	2.0
Hawaii	98.9	0.6
Idaho	31.9	0.2
Illinois	585.1	3.5
Indiana	206.8	1.3
Iowa	131.5	0.8
Kansas	101.9	0.6
Kentucky	181.3	1.1
Louisiana	164.0	1.0

---

[4] Under the law, basic block grant amounts for each state are the same as provided for in the original 1996 welfare reform law (P.L. 104-193). The national total state grant and each state's individual grant in the original TANF law is based on the federal share of expenditures in the pre-1996 AFDC, Emergency Assistance (EA), and Job Opportunities and Basic Skills (JOBS) training programs. The original formula entitled each state to the greatest of the average federal share of expenditures in these programs for FY1992 through FY1994; the federal share of expenditures for these programs in FY1994, adjusted for states that amended their EA programs in FY1994 or FY1995; or the federal share of expenditures for these programs in FY1995. The FY1994 adjustment for EA program amendments is the amount by which the federal share of EA expenditures in FY1995 exceeded that of FY1994.

State	Dollars in Millions	Percent of Total, 50 States and District of Columbia
Maine	78.1	0.5
Maryland	229.1	1.4
Massachusetts	459.4	2.8
Michigan	775.4	4.7
Minnesota	268.0	1.6
Mississippi	86.8	0.5
Missouri	217.1	1.3
Montana	45.5	0.3
Nebraska	58.0	0.4
Nevada	44.0	0.3
New Hampshire	38.5	0.2
New Jersey	404.0	2.5
New Mexico	126.1	0.8
New York	2,442.9	14.8
North Carolina	302.2	1.8
North Dakota	26.4	0.2
Ohio	728.0	4.4
Oklahoma	148.0	0.9
Oregon	167.9	1.0
Pennsylvania	719.5	4.4
Rhode Island	95.0	0.6
South Carolina	100.0	0.6
South Dakota	21.9	0.1
Tennessee	191.5	1.2
Texas	486.3	2.9
Utah	76.8	0.5
Vermont	47.4	0.3
Virginia	158.3	1.0
Washington	404.3	2.5
West Virginia	110.2	0.7
Wisconsin	318.2	1.9
Wyoming	21.8	0.1
Total 50 States and District of Columbia	16,488.7	100.0

Source: Congressional Research Service (CRS), based on data from the U.S. Department of Health and Human Services (HHS).

Note: State family assistance grants and MOE amounts are before reductions for allocations to tribal TANF programs operating in the state.

Supplemental Grants

During consideration of legislation that led to the 1996 law, fixed funding based on historic expenditures was thought to disadvantage two groups of states: (1) those that had relatively high population growth and (2) those that had historically low welfare grants relative to poverty in the state. Therefore, additional funding in the form of supplemental grants was provided to states that met criteria of high population growth and/or low historic grants per poor person. A total of 17 states qualified for supplemental grants: Alabama, Alaska, Arizona, Arkansas, Colorado, Florida, Georgia, Idaho, Louisiana, Mississippi, Montana, Nevada, New Mexico, North Carolina, Tennessee, Texas, and Utah.

For FY2001 through FY2010, supplemental grants were funded at $319 million per year. In FY2011, TANF supplemental grants were funded only through June 30, 2011. No funding for supplemental grants was provided for FY2012, FY2013, or FY2014.

Contingency Fund

The fixed basic grant under TANF also led to concerns that funding might be inadequate during economic downturns. The 1996 welfare reform law established a $2 billion "regular" TANF contingency fund.[5] To draw upon contingency funds, a state must both (1) meet a test of economic "need" and (2) spend from its own funds more than what the state spent in FY1994 on cash, emergency assistance, and job training in TANF's predecessor programs.

For purposes of the TANF contingency fund, a state meets the "economic need" test if

- its seasonally adjusted unemployment rate averaged over the most recent three-month period is at least 6.5% *and* at least 10% higher than its rate in the corresponding three-month period in either of the previous two years; *or*

- its Supplemental Nutrition Assistance Program (SNAP, formerly known as food stamps) caseload over the most recent three-month period is at least 10% higher than the adjusted caseload in the corresponding three-month period in FY1994 or FY1995. For this purpose, FY1994 and FY1995 caseloads are adjusted by subtracting out an estimate of participants who would have been made ineligible for food stamps (as the program was then named) under the 1996 welfare law had it been in effect in those years. The major group made ineligible was noncitizens.

Monthly payments from the contingency fund are limited to one-twelfth of 20% of a state's basic block grant, and states may receive these monthly payments on an advance basis. However, the

---

[5] P.L. 109-68, the TANF Emergency Response and Recovery Act of 2005, allowed states to draw upon the contingency fund to aid families evacuated from states damaged by Hurricane Katrina. States received 100% federal funding for families evacuated from a hurricane-damaged state to another host state. This was a temporary measure for the period September 2005 through August 2006. See CRS Report RS22246, *Temporary Assistance for Needy Families (TANF): Its Role in Response to the Effects of Hurricane Katrina*, by Gene Falk.

actual amount of contingency funds a state is entitled to for the year depends on (1) how much it spends in advance contingency funds and state funds over the FY1994 threshold, (2) its Medicaid matching rate, and (3) the number of months the state was eligible for contingency funds. A state's annual entitlement to contingency funds is calculated as the Medicaid matching rate times the state's extra spending (above FY1994 amounts) during the fiscal year, prorated by the number of months the state was eligible for contingency funds during the fiscal year.[6] A state that receives more in monthly advances from the contingency fund than it is entitled to for the year must remit overpayments to the federal treasury. A state may not receive more in contingency funds for the year than the total of its monthly advance payments, under an annual cap on contingency funds of 20% of the state's basic block grant.

The original $2 billion in this fund was depleted in early FY2010. For FY2009 and FY2010, states were able to draw additional TANF funds from a temporary "emergency" contingency fund (see CRS Report R41078, *The TANF Emergency Contingency Fund*, by Gene Falk). For FY2011 through FY2014, new funding for the TANF contingency fund has been provided in each year. For FY2013 and FY2014, P.L. 112-275 provided a $612 million appropriation for the contingency fund, though of this amount, $2 million was reserved in each year for a study on child abuse and neglect fatalities. Thus, $610 million was available for FY2013, and is available for FY2014, for TANF contingency fund grants.

State Funds: the Maintenance-of-Effort, or MOE, Requirement

TANF consolidated and replaced programs that provided matching grants to the states. Under the pre-TANF cash welfare program, federal funding was generally provided at the Medicaid matching rate (between 50% and 83%) to reimburse states for a share of their expenditures in the program.[7] This meant that there were considerable state dollars contributing to the pre-TANF programs. It also meant that the federal and state shares financing these programs varied by state, as the Medicaid matching rate is higher in states with lower per-capita incomes than higher per-capita incomes.

TANF requires states to maintain spending from their own funds on TANF or TANF-related activities. States are required in the aggregate to maintain at least $10.4 billion in spending on specified activities for needy families with children. The $10.4 billion, called the "maintenance-of-effort" (MOE) level, represents 75% of what was spent from state funds in FY1994 in TANF's predecessor programs of cash, emergency assistance, job training, and welfare-related child care spending.[8] States are required to maintain their own spending of at least that level, and the MOE

---

[6] For example, if a state was eligible for contingency funds for three months in a fiscal year, its proration factor would be one-fourth (three-twelfths). If it was eligible for contingency funds for six months in a fiscal year, its proration factor would be one-half (six-twelfths). A state eligible for contingency funds all year would not have its annual entitlement to funds prorated (i.e., it would receive the full amount).

[7] In the pre-1996 welfare law program, most administrative costs were reimbursed at a 50% rate (though some expenditures on data systems were reimbursed at a 90% rate). TANF also consolidated funding from two other programs: the Emergency Assistance program, which had a 50% matching rate, and the Job Opportunity and Basic Skills (JOBS) training program, which used the Medicaid matching rate but had a 60% (not 50%) minimum match.

[8] Some TANF MOE expenditures can also be counted toward meeting a separate child care "MOE" as part of the state spending requirements for the Child Care and Development Block Grant (CCDBG) matching grants. The maximum amount of funds that may be "double-counted" toward both the TANF and child care MOE requirements is $888 million, equal to the greater of FY1994 or FY1995 state expenditures in the pre-1996 child care programs. Analysis of combined federal and state funding or expenditures under the TANF and child care block grants must recognize that (continued...)

---

requirement increases to 80% of FY1994 spending for states that fail to meet TANF work participation requirements (discussed below). State expenditures under this requirement are often referred to as state MOE funds.

A state's failure to meet the MOE requirement results in a penalty. The penalty is a reduction in a state's subsequent year's block grant by $1 for each $1 shortfall from the required spending level.

Table 3 shows both federal TANF and state MOE funds. The MOE is shown at both the 75% and 80% rates for each state. Also shown is the percent of total federal and state funds in the TANF financial "system" that is accounted for by federal funds. This percentage varies because the Medicaid matching rate used in the pre-TANF programs varied by state. Mirroring the differences in federal shares under the pre-1996 programs, federal funds account for a greater share of total TANF funding in states with low per-capita income compared to those with higher per-capita income.

Table 3. Federal TANF and State MOE Funding Levels

(dollars in millions)

| State | Federal Basic Block Grant | State Maintenance of Effort (MOE) Funds | | Total Federal and State Funds at the 75% MOE Rate | Federal Funding as a Share of Total Federal and State Funding at the 75% MOE Rate |
		75% Rate	80% Rate		
Alabama	$93.3	$39.2	$41.8	$132.5	70.4%
Alaska	63.6	48.9	52.2	112.6	56.5
Arizona	222.4	95.0	101.4	317.4	70.1
Arkansas	56.7	20.8	22.2	77.6	73.1
California	3,733.8	2,726.9	2,908.7	6,460.7	57.8
Colorado	136.1	82.9	88.4	218.9	62.1
Connecticut	266.8	183.4	195.6	450.2	59.3
Delaware	32.3	21.8	23.2	54.1	59.7
District of Columbia	92.6	70.4	75.1	163.1	56.8
Florida	562.3	370.9	395.6	933.3	60.3
Georgia	330.7	173.4	184.9	504.1	65.6
Hawaii	98.9	73.0	77.8	171.9	57.5
Idaho	31.9	13.7	14.6	45.6	70.0

(...continued)

some state spending can be double-counted or it will overstate the amount of funding available or the amount of spending from the two block grants. The minimum amount of TANF MOE funds that cannot be double-counted toward CCDBG matching requirements is $9.5 billion.

State	Federal Basic Block Grant	State Maintenance of Effort (MOE) Funds		Total Federal and State Funds at the 75% MOE Rate	Federal Funding as a Share of Total Federal and State Funding at the 75% MOE Rate
		75% Rate	80% Rate		
Illinois	585.1	430.1	458.8	1,015.1	57.6
Indiana	206.8	113.5	121.1	320.3	64.6
Iowa	131.5	62.0	66.1	193.5	68.0
Kansas	101.9	61.7	65.9	163.7	62.3
Kentucky	181.3	67.4	71.9	248.7	72.9
Louisiana	164.0	55.4	59.1	219.4	74.7
Maine	78.1	37.5	40.0	115.6	67.6
Maryland	229.1	177.0	188.8	406.1	56.4
Massachusetts	459.4	358.9	382.9	818.3	56.1
Michigan	775.4	468.5	499.8	1,243.9	62.3
Minnesota	268.0	179.7	191.7	447.7	59.9
Mississippi	86.8	21.7	23.2	108.5	80.0
Missouri	217.1	120.1	128.1	337.2	64.4
Montana	45.5	15.7	16.8	61.2	74.3
Nebraska	58.0	28.6	30.5	86.7	67.0
Nevada	44.0	25.5	27.2	69.5	63.3
New Hampshire	38.5	32.1	34.3	70.6	54.5
New Jersey	404.0	300.2	320.2	704.2	57.4
New Mexico	126.1	37.3	39.8	163.4	77.2
New York	2,442.9	1,718.7	1,833.2	4,161.6	58.7
North Carolina	302.2	154.2	164.5	456.4	66.2
North Dakota	26.4	9.1	9.7	35.5	74.4
Ohio	728.0	390.8	416.9	1,118.8	65.1
Oklahoma	148.0	61.3	65.3	209.3	70.7
Oregon	167.9	92.3	98.4	260.2	64.5
Pennsylvania	719.5	407.1	434.3	1,126.6	63.9
Rhode Island	95.0	60.4	64.4	155.4	61.2
South Carolina	100.0	35.9	38.3	135.9	73.6
South Dakota	21.9	8.8	9.4	30.7	71.4
Tennessee	191.5	82.8	88.3	274.3	69.8
Texas	486.3	236.7	251.4	723.0	67.3

| State | Federal Basic Block Grant | State Maintenance of Effort (MOE) Funds | | Total Federal and State Funds at the 75% MOE Rate | Federal Funding as a Share of Total Federal and State Funding at the 75% MOE Rate |
		75% Rate	80% Rate		
Utah	76.8	25.3	27.0	102.1	75.2
Vermont	47.4	25.5	27.3	72.9	65.0
Virginia	158.3	128.2	136.7	286.5	55.3
Washington	404.3	272.1	290.2	676.4	59.8
West Virginia	110.2	32.3	34.4	142.5	77.3
Wisconsin	318.2	169.2	180.5	487.4	65.3
Wyoming	21.8	10.7	11.4	32.4	67.1
Total 50 States and District of Columbia	16,488.7	10,434.8	11,129.3	26,923.5	61.2

Source: Table prepared by CRS based on information from HHS.

Note: State family assistance grants and MOE amounts are before reductions for allocations to tribal TANF programs operating in the state.

TANF Benefits, Services, and Activities

Congress decided that TANF was to be named a "block grant" program. In public finance lingo, a block grant is a grant-in-aid given to states and local governments to address "broad purposes." Block grants also typically give governmental entities discretion in both defining problems and expending funds to address them. In a general sense, TANF meets this definition of a block grant, but its financing is complex (discussed above), and it does attach some "strings" to a state's use of TANF funds (discussed below).[9]

Using Federal TANF Grants

Federal TANF grants may be used for a wide range of benefits and services for families with children. Grants may be used within a state TANF program or transferred to either the Child Care and Development Block Grant (CCDBG) or the Social Services Block Grant (SSBG). Unused TANF funds can also be reserved (saved), without fiscal year limit.[10]

---

[9] For a general discussion of block grants, see CRS Report R40486, *Block Grants: Perspectives and Controversies*, by Robert Jay Dilger and Eugene Boyd.

[10] Before the enactment of the American Recovery and Reinvestment Act of 2009 (ARRA, P.L. 111-5), reserved funds (continued...)

Achieving TANF Goals

TANF allows states to expend funds "in any manner that is reasonably calculated" to achieve its statutory purpose within its state TANF program. TANF's purpose is to increase state flexibility to meet specified goals. Its four statutory goals are to

1. provide assistance to needy families so that children can be cared for in their own homes or in the homes of relatives;

2. end dependence of needy parents on government benefits through work, job preparation, and marriage;

3. reduce the incidence of out-of-wedlock pregnancies; and

4. promote the formation and maintenance of two-parent families.

The four goals of TANF encompass what is usually thought of as traditional cash welfare (assistance to families) and work activities for cash welfare families. However, the goals also provide authority for states to use funds for a wide variety of benefits and services for welfare families and other low-income families with children. States use TANF funds to help support work for low-income families through providing child care or transportation aid. The authority to provide assistance to care for children in the homes of relatives has been used by states to provide benefits and services to children and families of children who have been, or are at risk of, neglect or abuse and are placed in the care of a relative (e.g., grandparent, aunt, uncle). Further, TANF funds have been used for programs and services aimed at accomplishing the "family formation" goals of TANF (goals three and four listed above, and ending dependence through marriage, which is a component of goal two).

"Grandfathered" Activities

In addition to using funds to promote the purpose and goals of TANF, federal law allows states to use TANF funds to carry out any program or activity that a state had conducted under its pre-1996 programs. This provision permits states to continue activities they undertook under the pre-1996 Emergency Assistance (EA) program to provide help for foster care, adoption assistance,[11] and juvenile justice programs.

Transfers to Other Block Grants

Federal law allows up to 30% of federal TANF grants (except contingency funds) to be transferred to the CCDGB and SSBG combined, with a separate limit of 10% of TANF grants (except contingency funds) that may be transferred to SSBG.[12] Funds transferred to these other

---

(...continued)

could only be used for the purpose of providing "assistance" (often, cash welfare). The ARRA eliminated this restriction to the use of reserve funds, so that reserve funds can be used to provide any allowed TANF benefit or service.

[11] These would be foster care and adoption assistance cases that are ineligible for other federal financing from programs under Title IV-E of the Social Security Act.

[12] The original welfare reform law (P.L. 104-193) set the limit on transfers from TANF to SSBG at 10% of the TANF block grant. P.L. 105-178 (Transportation Equity Act for the 21st Century) reduced funding for SSBG and the transfer authority from TANF to SSBG to 4.25%, effective FY2001. However, annual appropriation bills and temporary (continued...)

---

block grants become subject to the rules of the receiving block grant (CCDBG or SSBG), and are not subject to TANF rules. However, TANF funds transferred to SSBG must be used for families with incomes below 200% of the poverty line.

Matching for Reverse Commuter Grants

Federal law also allows states to use federal TANF funds as a state match for reverse commuter grants. If a state makes use of federal TANF funds for this purpose, it is counted against the 30% limit for transfers to CCDBG and SSBG; that is, it reduces the amount of federal TANF funds that could be transferred to those other block grants.

Using State MOE Funds

Most, but not all, benefits, services, and activities that may be funded from federal TANF funds may also be financed by state MOE funds. States may count toward the MOE expenditures for *any* program that provides cash assistance, administration, child care, education, and training (though not educational activities for the general population), and other activities to further a TANF purpose. The major restrictions that apply to MOE (but not federal TANF) funds are

- for benefits, services, and activities that were not a part of the pre-1996 welfare law programs, expenditures count only to the extent that they exceed the FY1995 level of expenditure in the program; and

- expenditures on activities that were part of the pre-1996 welfare law programs that are not aimed to achieve a TANF goal ("grandfathered" activities) are not countable toward the MOE.

Table 4 provides a brief summary of the types of benefits, services, and activities that may be funded by federal TANF funds and with state MOE funds.[13]

(...continued)

extension legislation (that continued TANF on the terms of previous years) have provided for a 10% transfer limit for FY2001 and each subsequent fiscal year.

[13] Prior to the enactment of the Deficit Reduction Act of 2005 (DRA, P.L. 109-171) MOE funds used to achieve TANF's family formation goals were restricted to expenditures on "needy" families with children. The DRA had a provision that allows a state's total expenditure on activities to achieve these goals to be counted without regard to a family's need. However, HHS regulations issued on February 5, 2008, limit MOE expenditures related to the family formation goals except for activities related to promoting healthy marriage and responsible fatherhood. (See "Healthy Marriage and Responsible Fatherhood" later in this report for a listing of these activities.) For a discussion of this regulatory provision, see *Federal Register*, vol. 73, no. 24, p. 6517-6318.

Table 4. Summary of Rules for the Use of Federal TANF and State MOE Funds

May States Use Funds for ...	Federal TANF Funds	MOE Funds
Cash welfare, administration of cash welfare, and work programs?	Yes	Yes
Child care?	Yes, either through transfer to the Child Care and Development Block Grant (CCDBG), up to 30% of the grant, or within TANF.	Yes. States may not count child care funds spent for the state match for CCDBG matching funds, but may count up to $888 million spent toward the CCDBG MOE and any additional child care spending.
Activities to help achieve TANF family formation goals?	Yes	Yes, though under regulations many of these expenditures are limited to families that meet a need-test. Only expenditures on activities that seek to promote healthy marriage or responsible fatherhood may be available to the general population without a need-test.
Other benefits and services to help achieve TANF goals?	Yes	If activity was not authorized in pre-1996 programs, expenditures in ongoing programs only count if above FY1995 levels.
Activities in the pre-1996 welfare programs that are not reasonably calculated to help achieve TANF goals ("Grandfathered" activities)?	Yes	No

Source: Table prepared by CRS.

TANF Requirements for States

As discussed above, TANF provides states with broad authority to spend federal and MOE funds on a wide range of benefits and services. Though TANF is a block grant, there are some strings attached to states' use of funds, particularly with regard to families receiving "assistance" (essentially cash welfare). As discussed below, TANF funds used for benefits and services that are not considered assistance are generally free of most requirements.

Rules When Funds Are Used to Provide Assistance

Federal law specified that most TANF requirements apply only with respect to families receiving *assistance*. Federal TANF law does not define "assistance." However, HHS defines assistance in regulation as payment to families to meet "ongoing basic needs" such as food, clothing, shelter, utilities, household goods, personal care items, and other personal expenses.[14] Generally, such payments correspond to what most call cash welfare. Further, the regulations define TANF assistance to *include* child care and transportation aid for *nonworking* persons. Child care and transportation for *working* parents are explicitly *excluded* from the definition of assistance.

---

[14] The regulatory definition of assistance is found at 45 C.F.R. §260.31.

TANF Program and Separate State Programs

As discussed above, states may count their expenditures *in any program* toward meeting the MOE requirement. Programs other than TANF that contribute toward the MOE are known as "separate state programs." **Table 5** summarizes the application of TANF requirements for assistance recipients based on whether a benefit was financed from federal funds, state funds within the "TANF program," or separate state programs. Before FY2007, the major distinction in the rules for using state MOE funds under TANF and separate state programs was that the TANF work participation standards and child support requirements did not apply to families in separate state programs. Beginning in FY2007, work participation standards do apply to families in a separate state program. This leaves the major distinction that child support requirements do not apply to states for families in separate state programs.

**Table 5. Summary of TANF Requirements that Apply
to Recipients of Assistance, by Funding Source of the Benefit**

TANF Requirement	Federal TANF Funds	State Funds Expended in the "TANF Program"	Separate State Programs
Work participation standards	Yes	Yes	Beginning in FY2007, yes
Time limit	Yes	No	No
Prohibition for noncitizens during the first five years in the country	Yes	No	No
Assignment of child support to the state	Yes	Yes	No

Source: Table prepared by CRS.

Federal Eligibility Rules for Assistance

TANF requires that a family have a minor child to be eligible for assistance, including ongoing cash welfare. TANF defines a minor child as a person under the age of 18 or age 18 and still in school. Childless individuals and couples are not eligible for TANF assistance, except that assistance can be provided to a family with a pregnant woman. Additionally, a family receiving assistance must be *needy*—that is, have income below a specified level, though the level is determined by the state.

Federal law also prohibits states from using federal TANF funds to provide assistance to the following persons and families:

- families with an adult who has received federally funded aid for 60 months (see "The TANF Time Limit," discussed later in this report);

- unwed teen parents, unless living in an adult-supervised setting;

- teens who have not completed high school, unless they are making satisfactory progress toward achieving a high school or equivalent credential or in an alternative training program;

- noncitizens who arrived in the United States after August 22, 1996, for the first five years after arrival;[15]

- fugitive felons and parole violators; and

- persons convicted of a drug-related felony, unless the state affirmatively opts out of this provision.[16]

States that misuse federal TANF funds and assist such persons or families are penalized through a reduction in their block grant. However, states may provide assistance to these persons and families using MOE funds.

Aside from the requirement that TANF assistance be restricted to needy families with children and the listed statutory prohibitions on the use of federal funds, states have broad leeway to define eligibility for TANF cash assistance. States determine actual income eligibility standards (to determine whether a family is needy) and can determine other conditions and criteria for eligibility. States also determine benefit amounts paid to families.

In certain cases, the parent or caretaker relative is ineligible for assistance, but the children in their care are eligible. In these cases, benefits are paid on behalf of the children only; there is technically no adult recipient. These are known as "child-only" families receiving TANF assistance. The most common forms of "child-only" families are those where the parent is a recipient of Supplemental Security Income (SSI), the parent is a noncitizen ineligible for TANF assistance, or the child is being cared for by a nonparent caretaker relative (e.g., grandparent, aunt, or uncle).

TANF Work Requirements

TANF requires *states* to

- **assess each adult recipient's or teen parent's skills, work experience, and employability.** The assessment is required to be made within 90 days of determination of the recipient's eligibility for assistance.

- **engage each parent or caretaker adult in "work," as defined by the state, within 24 months of his or her coming on the rolls.** For this requirement, the state is free to determine what constitutes being engaged in work.[17]

- **sanction a family with a member who refuses to comply with its work requirements without "good cause."** States are free to determine the sanction amount, and whether to reduce benefits or terminate benefits for families that fail to comply with work requirements (a full-family sanction). States also determine what constitutes "good cause" for not complying with work requirements. States are prohibited from sanctioning a family with a single parent with a child under

---

[15] This prohibition is not found in TANF law itself, but was enacted in Title IV of the 1996 welfare law (P.L. 104-193), which generally set rules for noncitizens' access to publicly funded benefits.

[16] This prohibition is also not in TANF law itself, but was enacted in Section 115 of the 1996 welfare law (P.L. 104-193), and applies to both TANF and the Supplemental Nutrition Assistance Program (SNAP).

[17] This requirement is a part of the TANF state plan, and there is no specific penalty for a state that fails to engage a parent or caretaker in work by the 24-month deadline.

the age of six if he or she refuses to comply with work requirements because he or she cannot find affordable child care.

- **meet numerical work participation standards.** TANF sets minimum work participation standards that a state must meet. The standards are performance measures computed in the aggregate for each state, which require that a specified percentage of families be considered engaged in specified activities for a minimum number of hours. States are also required to have systems in place to verify work participation of individual recipients.

The work participation standards apply to states, not individual recipients. Work requirements applicable to individuals, and the financial sanctions on families with individuals who fail to comply with them, are determined by the states. States have considerable latitude in designing work requirements that apply to individuals, as long as the state meets its numerical participation standard.

Federal TANF Work Standard

To comply with TANF requirements, a state must meet two standards each year—the "all-family" and the "two-parent" family participation standards. The standards are that (1) 50% of *all* families and (2) 90% of *two-parent* families must meet participation standards. These statutory standards are reduced by "credits" that vary by state and by year. States receive credits for caseload reduction and for spending state funds in excess of what is required under the MOE.

TANF statute includes a caseload reduction credit. The caseload reduction credit reduces the 50% and 90% standards for a state by one percentage point for each percent decline in the cash assistance caseload from FY2005 levels.[18] A state is not given a credit for caseload reduction attributable to more restrictive policy changes made since FY2005.

Under HHS regulations promulgated in 1999, a state may also receive credits for spending in excess of what it is required to spend under the MOE requirement.[19] A state may consider families assisted by excess MOE as "caseload reduction," and hence receive extra caseload reduction credits for such families.

For example, if a state receives a 25 percentage point credit for caseload reduction and excess MOE spending, the statutory all-family standard of 50% is reduced by 25 percentage points—from 50% to 25%. In this example, a state's "effective standard" is 25%. If a state receives a credit of 50 percentage points for caseload reduction and excess MOE spending, its all-family standard is reduced by 50 percentage points—from 50% to 0%.

The TANF Work Participation Rate

To determine compliance with TANF federal work standards, a "work participation rate" is computed and then compared to a state's effective participation standard (i.e., statutory standard

---

[18] Before FY2007, a state was given a caseload reduction credit of one percentage point for each percent decline in the TANF caseload that occurred from its FY1995 (pre-welfare reform) level.

[19] These regulations are at 45 C.F.R. §261.43.

reduced by credits). The TANF work participation rate represents the percent of non-excluded families receiving assistance who are considered "engaged in work" during a fiscal year.[20]

Families Included in the Participation Rate Calculation

Only families with a "work-eligible" individual are included in the calculation of the TANF work participation rate. Under TANF, work-eligible persons are either adult recipients of cash assistance or certain non-recipient parents of children receiving assistance who are expected to work. The adults in most categories of "child-only" TANF families are not included in the participation rate calculation, and hence most "child-only" families are excluded from the participation rate.

The following adults in TANF or MOE-funded households are *not* considered work-eligible:

- adult non-recipients who are non-parent caretakers (e.g., grandparent, aunt, uncle);

- ineligible noncitizen parents;

- at state option, parents receiving Supplemental Security Income (SSI);[21]

- parents who are needed in the home to care for disabled family members;

- at state option, parents who are Social Security Disability Insurance (SSDI) recipients; and

- at state option, a parent who became eligible for SSI during the fiscal year.

Additionally, states may exclude from the calculation of the work participation rate: (1) single parents caring for an infant, though this exclusion is limited to 12 months in a recipient's lifetime; (2) families being sanctioned, though this exclusion is limited to 3 months in a 12-month period; and (3) families participating in tribal TANF programs.

"Engaged in Work"

Work-eligible individuals must participate in specific activities during a month for a state to count them as "engaged in work" and have the activities count toward the work participation standard. Work-eligible individuals must also participate in activities for a minimum number of hours per week in a month to be considered "engaged in work." In general, single parents with a pre-school aged child (under the age of six) must participate for at least 20 hours per week in a month; other single parents must participate at least 30 hours per week in a month. Two-parent families must participate for more hours to be counted as engaged in work.

---

[20] Under the TANF statute, a participation rate is calculated for each month. The fiscal year participation rate is the (simple) average of the participation rates for each month.

[21] Before October 1, 2006, all families without an adult recipient were excluded from the work participation rate calculation. The Deficit Reduction Act of 2005 (P.L. 109-171) required HHS to issue regulations to determine the circumstances under which a family with a non-recipient parent must be included in the work participation rate calculation. The HHS regulations generally require that states *include* the following types of families without an adult recipient in the work participation rate calculation: (1) except for three months in a 12-month period, families subject to a sanction that removes the adult from the TANF assistance unit; and (2) families that reach state time limits that remove the adult from the TANF assistance unit but continue aid on behalf of the family's children.

Most welfare-to-work activities are on the list of 12 activities that count toward the participation standards, including educational and rehabilitative activities. The statute lists the 12 activities; the Deficit Reduction Act of 2005 (P.L. 109-171) required HHS to define each of the 12 activities. **Table 6** shows the 12 TANF work activities and their regulatory definitions.

Table 6. Countable TANF Work Activities and Their Definitions

Activity	Definition
Unsubsidized employment	Full- or part-time employment in the public or private sector that is not subsidized by TANF or any other public program.
Subsidized private sector employment	Employment in the private sector for which the employer receives a subsidy from TANF or other public funds to offset some or all of the wages and costs of employing an individual.
Subsidized public sector employment	Employment in the public sector for which the employer receives a subsidy from TANF or other public funds to offset some or all of the wages and costs of employing an individual.
Job search and readiness *Participation in this activity may be counted for 6 weeks (12 weeks in certain circumstances) in a fiscal year.*	The act of seeking or obtaining employment, or preparation to seek or obtain employment, including life-skills training and substance abuse treatment, mental health treatment, or rehabilitation activities. Such treatment or therapy must be determined to be necessary and documented by a qualified medical, substance abuse, or mental health professional.
Community service	Structured programs and embedded activities in which TANF recipients perform work for the direct benefit of the community under the auspices of public or nonprofit organizations. Community service programs must be limited to projects that serve a useful community purpose in fields such as health, social service, environmental protection, education, urban and rural redevelopment, welfare, recreation, public facilities, public safety, and child care. A state agency shall take into account, to the extent possible, the prior training, experience, and skills of an individual in making appropriate community service assignments.
Work experience	A work activity, performed in return for welfare that provides an individual with an opportunity to acquire the general skills, knowledge, and work habits necessary to obtain employment. The purpose of work experience is to improve the employability of an individual who cannot find unsubsidized full-time employment.
On-the-job training	Training in the public or private sector that is given to a paid employee while he or she is engaged in productive work and that provides knowledge and skills essential to the full and adequate performance of the job.
Vocational educational training *Participation in this activity is limited to 12 months in a lifetime.*	Organized educational programs that are directly related to the preparation of individuals for employment in current or emerging occupations.
Caring for a child of a recipient in community service	Providing child care to enable another cash welfare recipient to participate in a community services program. This is an unpaid activity and must be a structured program to improve the employability of participating individuals.
Job skills training directly related to employment	Training or education for job skills required by an employer to provide an individual with the ability to obtain employment or to advance or adapt to the changing demands of the workplace.
Education directly related to employment (for those without a high school or equivalent degree)	Education related to a specific occupation, job, or job offer.

Activity	Definition
Completion of a secondary school program (for those without a high school or equivalent degree)	In the case of a recipient who has not completed secondary school or received such a certificate, this means regular attendance, in accordance with the requirements of a secondary school or course of study, at a secondary school or in a course of study leading to a certificate of general equivalence.

Source: Table prepared by CRS based on HHS regulations. See *Federal Register*, vol. 73, no. 24, February 5, 2008, pp. 6772-6828.

There are limits on the ability of states to count participation in pre-employment activities such as education, rehabilitative activities, and job search toward the work standards:

- For work-eligible individuals age 20 and older, participation in a GED program counts only if the recipient also participates in activities more closely related to work for at least 20 hours per week.[22] Vocational educational training may be counted only for 12 months in a recipient's lifetime.

- The combination of job search and rehabilitative activities (e.g., rehabilitation from a disability, substance abuse treatment) is limited to a maximum of 12 weeks in a fiscal year.

Penalties for States that Fail the Work Participation Standard

A state that fails to meet TANF work participation standards is penalized by a reduction in its block grant. The penalty is a 5% reduction in the block grant for the first year's failure to meet the standard, and increased by 2 percentage points each year (that is, a total reduction of 7% in the second year and 9% in the third year, etc.), up to a maximum penalty of 21%.

However, the law requires that this penalty be based "on the degree of noncompliance." Thus, actual penalties may be lower than the amounts set in statute. Further, penalties may be reduced if a state is in recession (based on the contingency fund's indicators of an economically needy state; see "Contingency Fund," earlier in this report) or if the noncompliance was due to "extraordinary circumstances, such as a natural disaster or regional recession." Additionally, penalty relief is granted to a state that has failed to comply with participation standards because of waivers of program requirements provided to victims of domestic violence (see "Special Provisions for Victims of Domestic Violence," later in this report).

Verifying Work Participation

States are required to have procedures to verify recipients' work participation: identifying who is subject to or excluded from work standards; how a recipient's activities represent countable TANF work activities; and how to count and verify reported hours of work. HHS regulations require that descriptions of these procedures be included in a state work verification plan. States that fail to comply with these work verification requirements are subject to a penalty of between 1% and 5% of the state's block grant.

---

[22] Teen parents (under the age of 20) may be deemed "engaged in work" through completing high school or obtaining a General Educational Development (GED) diploma.

The TANF Time Limit

States may not use federal TANF funds to provide assistance to a family containing an adult who has received five years (60 months) of assistance. The federal TANF time limit does not apply to families without an adult recipient, the "child-only" cases.

The federal five-year time limit is a prohibition on states' use of federal TANF funds, not a direct limitation on how long a particular family may receive welfare. How time limits affect families is determined by states, which have wide latitude in implementing them.

Federal law provides a hardship exception to the time limit, allowing federal funds to be used in cases of hardship for up to 20% of the caseload beyond the five-year limit. Further, federal law explicitly allows a state to use state MOE funds to aid a family beyond the time limit.

TANF penalizes states that have more than 20% of their caseload on the rolls for more than five years. The penalty is a 5% reduction in the block grant. Many states have adopted the five-year limit as their own; others have shorter time limits. Some states effectively do not limit the amount of time a family may receive assistance.

Child Support Enforcement Requirements

Families receiving cash assistance are often headed by a single mother. In most of these families, there is a noncustodial parent who is also likely to be financially responsible for the children's economic well-being.

Families receiving TANF assistance must cooperate with certain child support enforcement requirements. They must cooperate with the state in establishing the paternity of a child and in establishing, modifying, or enforcing orders that the noncustodial parent pay child support. Federal law requires states to penalize families who do not cooperate with child support enforcement requirements by cutting their benefits at least 25%. States could penalize families by more, and even end assistance for failure to cooperate with child support enforcement requirements.

Families receiving TANF assistance must assign (legally turn over) any child support they receive from noncustodial parents to their state as a reimbursement for welfare costs. The federal government and the states split the receipts from assigned child support. A state has the option of passing through assigned child support to TANF families. The federal government shares in the cost of passing through child support paid to TANF families as long as the child support is also disregarded in determining TANF eligibility and benefit amounts.[23] State expenditures from the pass-through of child support, if disregarded in determining a welfare family's benefit, are countable toward the TANF MOE.

---

[23] The amount of the pass-through that the federal government will share the cost of is limited to $100 for a family with one child and $200 for families with two or more children. This is a provision of the Deficit Reduction Act of 2005. See CRS Report RS22377, *Child Support Provisions in the Deficit Reduction Act of 2005 (P.L. 109-171)*, by Carmen Solomon-Fears.

Special Provisions for Victims of Domestic Violence

Federal law provides for an optional certification that a state has procedures in place to screen for and identify victims of domestic violence, refer such victims to supportive services, and waive certain program requirements. The program requirements that may be waived include work requirements, the time limit, and cooperation with child support enforcement rules.

Though the state may waive certain program requirements for victims of domestic violence, federal law does not exclude them from the TANF work participation rate standard calculation or from the 20% limit on hardship cases that exceed the five-year time limit. However, HHS regulations allow a state to provide victims of domestic violence a federally recognized good cause domestic violence waiver, and provide that a state would have "good cause" for failing the requirements if that failure was due to providing such waivers.[24]

A federally recognized domestic violence waiver must identify program requirements that are being waived; be granted based on an individualized assessment; and be accompanied by a services plan. These waivers must be reassessed at least every six months.

Restrictions on Cash Withdrawals at Certain Establishments

States generally pay benefits by placing funds on Electronic Benefit Transaction (EBT) cards to be used by recipients making withdrawals from Automated Teller Machines (ATMs) or making purchases at point-of-sale terminals. Federal law requires states to maintain policies and practices to prevent TANF assistance funds from being used in an EBT transaction in liquor stores, casinos or gaming establishments, and strip clubs. States must prevent TANF cash withdrawals at ATMs in such establishments, and prevent purchases using TANF assistance on EBT cards at point-of-sale terminals in such establishments.

States have two years after the enactment of P.L. 112-96 (enacted February 22, 2012) to implement these policies. Additionally, TANF state plans are required to ensure that recipients (1) would have adequate access to their benefits; (2) would have access to their benefits at minimal fees or charges, including free access; and (3) are provided information on applicable fees and charges.

Rules When TANF or MOE Funds Are Used for Benefits and Services Other Than "Assistance"

As previously discussed, most TANF federal requirements relate to "assistance." However, TANF gives states permission to spend federal funds and count state spending toward the MOE on a wide range of benefits and services other than assistance. Essentially, TANF and MOE funds may be spent on benefits, services, or activities aimed to achieve any of the goals of TANF. Examples of such benefits and services include short-term, non-recurring aid,[25] child care for families with working members, transportation aid for families with working members, refundable tax credits

---

[24] See regulations at 45 C.F.R. §§260.50-260.59.

[25] Non-recurrent short-term aid is defined in regulations as benefits that (1) are designed to deal with a specific crisis situation or episode of need; (2) are not intended to meet recurrent or ongoing needs; and (3) will not extend beyond four months.

for working families with children,[26] funding of Individual Development Accounts (IDAs), education and training for low-income parents, and activities that seek to achieve the family formation goals (goals three and four) of TANF. Such benefits and services may be provided to families receiving assistance, but also might be provided to other families who have no connection to the cash welfare rolls.

State Accountability

Federal law gives states broad flexibility in designing and implementing state programs operated with TANF and MOE funds. It also requires states to develop plans that outline their intended use of funds and report data on families receiving assistance.

TANF State Plans

States are required to submit state plans every three years as a condition of receiving TANF block grant funds. The bulk of these plans is an "outline" of the program the state "intends" to operate. The Secretary of HHS cannot disapprove a state plan based on its content. Rather, the role of the Secretary is to determine whether the state has included information on all required elements of the plan. State plans have no set format, and vary greatly in their content and detail.

State plans are not required to have—and often do not have—information on basic financial and nonfinancial eligibility rules for TANF assistance. For example, a state is not required to provide information on income eligibility rules, treatment of earnings, or information on its time limit in the state plan. Some eligibility information is collected for programs funded with MOE dollars in annual program reports, but it is not of the detail necessary to describe, for example, the maximum amount of earnings a family may have and still remain eligible for TANF assistance.

Data Reporting

TANF law and regulations require states to provide information on families receiving assistance. States must provide both caseload counts and family- and recipient-level information on families receiving assistance. Family- and individual-level information that states must report includes basic demographic information, the work activities hours of adults, and the financial circumstances of families and individual recipients receiving assistance. Neither caseload counts nor characteristic information is required to be reported for families receiving TANF-funded benefits and services that are not considered assistance. P.L. 112-96 requires the Secretary of HHS to issue a rule to create standards for data required to be reported under TANF to better facilitate its exchange with other data systems.

---

[26] HHS regulations provide that refundable state earned income tax credits are not considered assistance. It should be noted that only the "refundable" portion of a state tax credit may be financed through either federal TANF or MOE funds. That is, the portion of the tax credit that exceeds a family's state tax liability and requires a payment (expenditure) from the state treasury may be financed via TANF. Tax credits that reduce a family's tax liability are not allowable uses of federal TANF funds nor are they countable toward the MOE.

Other TANF Provisions

Healthy Marriage and Responsible Fatherhood

The Deficit Reduction Act of 2005 created new TANF funding for healthy marriage promotion, Indian child welfare, and responsible fatherhood initiatives. An appropriation of $150 million per year was provided for each of five years (FY2006 through FY2010) for the following initiatives:

- up to $50 million per year may be used to fund "Responsible Fatherhood Initiatives" (see below);

- up to $2 million per year may be used to fund demonstration projects to test the effectiveness of Indian tribal governments in coordinating child welfare services to children at risk of abuse and neglect; and

- the remainder (a minimum of $98 million per year) is for demonstration projects and technical assistance on "Healthy Marriage Promotion Initiatives" (see below).

Beginning in FY2011, $75 million per year has been allocated for healthy marriage initiatives and $75 million per year has been allocated for responsible fatherhood initiatives. Any funds for tribal government child welfare coordination demonstrations would equally reduce the $75 million allocated to healthy marriage and responsible fatherhood initiatives.

Healthy Marriage Promotion Initiatives

The healthy marriage promotion initiative funds (1) awards by HHS to public or private entities to conduct research and demonstration projects; and (2) technical assistance to states, Indian tribes and tribal organizations, and other entities. The activities supported by these initiatives include

- programs to promote marriage in the general population, such as public advertising campaigns on the value of marriage and education in high schools on the value of marriage;

- education in "social skills" (e.g., marriage education, marriage skills, conflict resolution, and relationship skills); and

- programs that reduce the financial disincentives to marry, if combined with educational or other marriage promotion activities.

Applicants for marriage promotion grants must ensure that participation in such activities is voluntary and that domestic violence concerns are addressed (e.g., through consultations with experts on domestic violence).

Responsible Fatherhood Initiatives

Allowable activities under responsible fatherhood initiatives include those to promote marriage; teach parenting skills through counseling; mentoring, mediation, and dissemination of information; employment and job training services; media campaigns; and development of a national clearinghouse focused on responsible fatherhood.

Tribal TANF

Federally recognized Indian tribes and certain Alaskan Native organizations have the option to operate their own TANF programs for needy families with children. Tribes are entitled to receive a grant equal to the amount of FY1994 federal expenditures in pre-TANF programs attributable to Indian families residing in the area to be served by the tribal program. This is financed by a reduction in the state's block grant amount. States may, but are not required to, provide tribes with MOE funds.

Tribes seeking to operate TANF programs must submit plans to the Secretary of HHS for approval. The Secretary of HHS—with the participation of the tribes—establishes work requirements and time limits for each tribe operating its own TANF program.

Additionally, tribes that operated pre-TANF work and education programs are provided grants to operate tribal work programs that total $7.6 million per year. The amount of each grant equals what the tribe received in FY1994 under pre-TANF programs.

Research and Demonstration Funds

TANF law appropriates $15 million per year for research and evaluation activities for state TANF programs. (Before FY2002, these funds were annually rescinded in appropriations acts, with welfare-related research funded through another HHS research and evaluation account.) Half of these funds must be used for state-initiated research projects; the remainder is to be used for federally initiated projects.

Census Bureau Funds

TANF law also appropriates $10 million per year to the U.S. Census Bureau to fund a longitudinal survey of a representative sample of households to examine the effects of welfare reform. This survey is known as the Survey of Program Dynamics, and includes information on the sample for a 10-year period spanning 1992-2003.

Author Contact Information

Gene Falk
Specialist in Social Policy
gfalk@crs.loc.gov, 7-7344